Blue! Blue! You slow dog you!

Author and Illustrator:

Stephanie Snider

In dedication to Rylee Ann Fanning and her dog Blue.
An everlasting friendship

Rylee begins her hike by skipping out the front door, calling for her dog, Blue, to join her. As they make their way out of the yard and onto the trail, they hear Mother, "Don't be too long, dinner is nearly ready!" They look at each other with widened eyes and mutually growing hunger.

It is not long into the hike before Blue begins to do what a hound dog does best; sniff **anything** and **everything** in sight. He is quickly drawn off the trail by a curious aroma coming from the surrounding greens. He is on the search when he is startled by a loud voice, "Ah! Oh! Whew! Wait!"

Blue turns his head toward the loud yelling only to discover a **strange** looking creature on a leaf. This is the first time Blue has ever seen an animal such as this, so he introduces himself. "Hello, my name is Blue, and I am a hoouunnd dog. How are you? What is your name, friend?"

"Why, hello Blue, my name is Charlie the Caterpillar. So nice to meet you, but that nose of yours almost knocked me onto the ground. Would you **please** mind being more careful?" asked Charlie.

As Blue apologizes to Charlie for the disruption, he hears Rylee's voice faintly calling to him "Blue! Blue! You slow dog, you! Come on, catch up!"

Blue nods to Charlie and **scrambles** next to Rylee's side.
Once he reaches her, she reminds him that they must keep a steady
pace. "We cannot be late for dinner," she says. He delivers a long,
agreeable howl and continues to trot down the trail.

They approach a bridge, one that Blue remembers as scary. The creaks, the cracks, and the continuous swaying make Blue very uneasy. But not Rylee. Without hesitation or thought, she crosses over. She's even whistling as she does it! Blue watches, in wonder at her bravery. He works up the courage and puts one paw down on the bridge. His approach is much more cautious. As he takes his first step, he catches a scent in the air. He must find out where this yummy aroma is coming from!

He steps off the bridge and the trail, only to find himself submerged in the foliage once more. He knows this distracting, delightful scent is close. His nose sniffs up high and down low, eager to find this scent. Suddenly, there it was, a basket full of perfect carrots! His drooling has already begun. Blue leans forward to take one, when he notices something behind the basket.

"Oh!" It is a **bunny rabbit**, and not just any bunny rabbit, it's his old pal Reggie! He knows Reggie from the backyard. Blue shouts with glee, "Reggie! It is so good to see you. Where have you been?"

Reggie, with as much enthusiasm as possible having a mouthful of carrots, exclaims, "Mmmmmmmm, Mmmmmmmm, Mmmmmmmm! Crunch! Crunch! Crunch!" Blue looks confused by this reply, but knows it was spoken with the **warmest** regard.

Rylee is again calling, "Blue! Blue! You slow dog, you! Hurry, catch up!" His long ears perk up and he knows he must go. He smiles at the hungry rabbit to bid farewell, and **swiftly** moves back on track.

He is doing his best to catch up to Rylee, putting his fears of the bridge aside. Before he knows it, he is right back with her. Lucky for him, she stopped to admire the **vibrant** and **fragrant** wildflowers. This picture-perfect spot is their favorite place on the hike.

Rylee has an idea. "Let's pick a bouquet of flowers for Mother, as a gift," she says. She asks Blue to help her pick the most beautiful, colorful, and **sweet-scented flowers** to bring back home. Blue thought, "This was the best job I could ever have!" He gives a delighted nod and they start their search.

He is on patrol for only a few moments when a magnificent **butterfly** lands on his nose. He is a little scared at first, but is quickly calmed by a small, questioning voice. "You're a strange, smelly flower. Do you have a name? I have never seen a flower that drools, has such long ears, and big feet!" Blue *giggles* in reply. "I am not a flower! I am a basset hoouunnd." His answer ending with a baying howl.

The magnificent butterfly can sense Blue is silly, kind, and gentle, even though she is still unsure what a basset hound is, exactly. She introduces herself as **Butterfly Bree**. She tells him, "You are my most interesting friend." He returns the compliment to the graceful butterfly.

Blue's eyes begin to widen as he realizes he has once again found himself away from Rylee. He says goodbye to his small buddy and rushes to find his true best friend, Rylee.

As the two get closer and closer to home, Rylee confesses her hopes of spaghetti for dinner. This was their **favorite** pasta dish. Blue looks up at Rylee. At the thought of spaghetti, he gets twinkles in his droopy eyes and begins drooling shoestrings from both sides of his mouth. A **hungry grumble** comes from his tummy ... Oh boy! Spaghetti! Spaghetti! Oh boy!

Just before they reach the back door, Blue takes a few big **sniffs** of the air trying to uncover the unknown, what's for dinner? He turns his head to Rylee as he picks up the dinner scent. He starts to leap around in joy. With barely controlled excitement, Blue sprints toward the house, yelling, "It is spaghetti, Rylee! Oh boy! Oh boy! We're so lucky! **Spaghetti!!"** Then the two best friends head inside together to discuss their hiking adventure while dining on their favorite meal.

The End